OVER HERE

The American car in England in the 1960s

Volume 1

OVER HERE

The American car in England in the 1960s

Volume 1

Written and photographed by

Steve Miles

SGM
Publishing

ISBN 0-9545624-4-5

Printed in Great Britain by
The Bath Press

First published in Great Britain in 2004 by

SGM Publishing
Cosgrove Wharf, Lock Lane, Cosgrove, Northants MK19 7JR
info@sgmpublishing.co.uk

Introduction

IN 1959, my parents made the mistake of buying me a camera for Christmas. This was probably the result of the fact that I had appropriated their camera to my own use that summer, when we were on holiday in Devon, and taken great pleasure in the creation of the resultant fuzzy black-and-white images. That first camera was a simple, roll-film Coronet; as the years passed, I progressed to more sophisticated types, eventually switching to a 35mm single-lens-reflex late in 1964. I am still a keen photographer, member of my local camera clubs and an accredited club circuit judge.

Growing up in the City of Oxford, a town then surrounded by numerous outposts of the United States Air Force, and having a motor trade employee for a father, it was perhaps inevitable that I would develop a fascination with the spectacular products of the U.S. Automotive Industry, so wildly different from the Morris Oxfords, 100E Ford Populars and Hillman Minxes which otherwise populated our streets. Not to mention the annual treat, courtesy of Dad's employers, of a visit to the Earl's Court Motor Show, where the latest Detroit art-forms could be contrasted with the mundane output of European factories - Imagine the effect of a sparkling-new 1958 Buick, or the outlandishly radical style of the all-new Edsel, on a car-mad boy of ten!

It took no great leap of the intellect to combine these two interests. The result was that, from around 1962, I was normally to be found wandering the streets of Oxford, or hopping on the train or coach to London, in pursuit of American cars for my collection, rather like a sort of mechanically-besotted lepidopterist. My ambition, though never stated as such, was to spot and photograph an example of every make and model produced by my heroes of General Motors, Chrysler and Ford, not to mention American Motors and such prized rarities as Studebaker and Packard. This passion lasted for many years, past the end of my schooling and into my early years of employment in the Pharmaceutical Industry, in Hertfordshire, only petering out under the pressure of other interests (notably girls) as my horizons widened.

The end result, when I eventually plucked up the courage to investigate, is a collection of black-and-white negatives totalling around ten thousand (yes, 10,000), all of American cars on the streets of England between 1962 and about 1970. A friend pointed out not long ago that this could now be regarded as a historical document - sounds rather presumptuous, but I suppose he's right, in a way: It is a record not only of all those wonderful cars themselves, but of a time when the American car was a not-uncommon sight on our roads, when you could go into a London showroom and buy a brand-new Buick or a Lincoln, and when Ford Galaxies, Chevrolet Impalas and Pontiac Parisiennes came with right-hand-drive. Who else out there remembers

Lendrum and Hartmann, and the plush new showroom in Flood Street which they moved to from the dinginess of Albemarle Street, round the back of Piccadilly? Or Simpson's of Wembley, or Lincoln Cars, out in Brentford?

Anyway, dear reader, here it is. The first volume of my collected photographs - given that number of available negatives, you may justifiably guess that there could be more to come in the future. If the selection of the images that follow appears almost random, that is because, in large part, it is. With that many available pictures, you might imagine that I could easily produce a volume each for every one of the then-extant US car manufacturers – possible, certainly, but to have tried to do so would have involved such an enormous amount of work, sifting, selecting and listing, that the appearance of this first volume would have been delayed by many months, if not years. I have rather chosen to start with that part of my later, 35mm, collection, which was shot in the Greater London area, and to simply approach each negative file, select from it those images which I consider to be of sufficient interest to be reproduced herein, and transfer those pictures by the miracle of computer technology into a form suitable for publication.

I make no apology for this, nor for the fact that you will find herein not only the rare, the expensive, the spectacular, but also the relatively mundane, the cheap, the truly ordinary models which the less well off US citizen was wont to purchase - the kind of thing which is now the rarity on the rally fields! Nor have I attempted to 'clean up' these images too much – the negatives are around forty years old, and some are showing their age, I agree, but I didn't want to make them appear too 'modern'. Just reframing, to give the cars themselves just prominence, and a little judicious adjusting of brightness and contrast. And of course film technology has come a long way in the forty years that have passed since these pictures were taken – some of the images which follow were shot on high-speed films, with the inherent graininess that results, and others were shot at rather long range, and, to make them comprehensible have now been enlarged from a small part of the negative, adding further to that effect. But I hope the overall selection will appeal to other lovers of the classic American car – there are, I know, many gaps; but hopefully later selections from my collection will begin to fill these in.

You will also discover that not all of the cars illustrated between these covers are in pristine, showroom condition. I have always had a thing about originality, so most of what you are about to see are cars that are complete and unmodified, but a few of them are showing definite signs of wear and tear. You have to remember that what I was photographing were cars in everyday use, not the pampered collectors pieces we see on today's rally fields, and many of them were even then ten or fifteen years old.

I hope the pictures in this volume give you as much pleasure as they did me, both at the time of taking, and more recently as I have gone back over them preparatory to sharing them with you. If you have enjoyed this volume, if it has whetted your appetite for more, rest assured that I am even now beginning to work on the next selection from my collection – and there are still all the older roll-film negatives, to be looked at!

Steve Miles
September 2004

Plate 1 **1946 Buick Special.** Chance, and the Roman alphabet, conspire to make the first illustration of this book also the earliest car to be included. In common with all US manufacturers, GM began post-war production with little-changed versions of what had been all-new 1942 models – very early production cars lacked any bright trim, as a result of a shortage of materials, so it is interesting to note the silver-painted grille and bumpers of this car. The Special remained, as it had been since the mid-thirties, Buick's lowest-priced model.

Plate 2 **1956 Buick Super.** Buick's pre-war model line-up continued for more than ten years after the return of peace – the Super and Roadmaster were the high-price cars, built on the bigger C-body shell shared with Cadillac. The Super's 255 bhp, 322 cid V8 was developed from the engine first introduced to replace the aging straight eights, for which Buick had been famous, in 1953. This slightly tatty example was spotted in a Soho backstreet.

Plate 3 **1958 Buick Century.** The Century, first introduced in 1937, was Buick's entry in the 'performance' field – the smaller, lighter Special body and chassis was fitted with the higher-output engine of the Super, to give a car which offered more urge in a fairly agile package. Buick's 1958 models shared GM's unfortunate corporate decision to run with all-new body shells every year – unfortunate in that it coincided with the worst sales year since the war. This one, missing its right-hand parking light, was photographed in the forecourt of an Earls Court apartment block.

Plate 4 **1959 Buick Electra.** 1959, in line with the decision mentioned above, saw all-new models across the board once again; that year also saw the final demise of the traditional Buick model names. Lower-price cars were now called LeSabre and Invicta, as before based on the smaller B-body, with the Electra models sharing Cadillac's C-body along with the Oldsmobile 98. Styling had changed from the heavily-ornamented to the highly-exuberant – this is the regular pillared sedan.

Plate 5   **1959 Buick Electra 225.** Top-of-the-line in Buick's new listing was the Electra 225, with the highest level of trim and equipment. Available only as a convertible or four-door hardtop, as here, 225's can be identified by their more elaborate rocker-panel trim – the four-door, shown here, carried the now-infamous 'flat-top' roof shared across the GM line-up, in contrast to the regular pillared sedan in plate 4.

Plate 6   **1960 Buick Invicta.** With the ill-fated 'new body every year' policy now forgotten, 1960 GM cars wore restyled 1959 shells. Buick for 1960 showed pared-down fins, still slanted at a dramatic 45 degrees, and headlamps moved from the tilt into pods which resembled those housing the paired jet engines of Boeing's new B52 – this Invicta was the cheapest convertible in the line-up.

Plate 7   **1961 Buick LeSabre.** The new body-shells for 1961 went for a much sleeker look, with long, low lines and sculptured sides. Buick's model range remained the same, except for the reappearance of the Special nameplate on their new entry in the compact car market – this LeSabre two-door hardtop was spotted in an underground car park near the American Embassy in Grosvenor Square.

Plate 8   **1962 Buick Electra 225.** 1962 saw a rationalisation of Buick's high-price cars, with the dropping of the plain Electra nameplate, and the expansion of the 225 models to a full range of body styles – in this case, the pillared four-door sedan, captured en passant on Park Lane where the one-way circuit loops around at the Southern end, which was one of my favourite spots to lay in wait for my prey – this backdrop may become quite familiar!

Plate 9   1962 Buick Invicta. Buick's 1962 restyling made the best of the current body shells, with a result which was both attractive and distinctive. Unusually, a new roofline was introduced on this two-door hardtop, mimicking the appearance of a convertible. This less-than-shiny car was captured in a sidestreet off of Kensington High Street.

Plate 10   1963 Buick LeSabre.   The two-door LeSabre sedan was the cheapest full-size Buick you could buy, and the only one to come in at less than three thousand dollars; this four-door was but a few dollars more! The new styling was in line with the fashion of the time, being composed of long straight lines, but managed somehow to look more cumbersome than the trim 62's.

Plate 11   1963 Buick Electra 225. Still based on the big C-body shell, the 1963 Electra 225 became more distinctive from the lower-priced lines, with razor-edged rear-end styling completely different from the LeSabre and Wildcat, which had replaced the Invicta as the mid-price model. For those who may be wondering, RUV stands for the Republic of the Upper Volta, which I believe is a small state in West Africa; their embassy, outside which I found the car, was then in Portland Place.

Plate 12   1963 Buick Riviera. New to Buick's line-up for 1963 was the Riviera, a two-door hardtop coupe with these delightfully sleek lines and a luxurious four-seat interior. Aimed squarely at Ford's successful Thunderbird, the Riviera was an immediate sales hit itself, with some forty thousand being produced in the first year, barely less than the hardtop T-Bird.

Plate 13 **1964 Buick Skylark.** First introduced for 1961, Buick's compact Special had quickly spawned the up-market Skylark, firstly as a two-door only 'sporty' model, but by 1964 as a full line-up of body types. An all-new A-body shell that year took the Special/Skylark, along with the equivalent models from Oldsmobile and Pontiac, up into a new 'intermediate' category between the traditional full-size cars and the compacts. The scenery here will be seen again – a different angle of view from my vantage point on Park Lane, not far from the Hilton Hotel, as in Plate 8.

Plate 14 **1965 Buick Skylark.** The smaller Buicks for 1965 were only mildly face-lifted from the 1964 models, with heavier bumpers and revised rear lights. Engine options were a V6, derived from the now-abandoned aluminium-block V8 but made of cast iron, or the small (300 cid) iron V8.

Plate 15   1965 Buick Skylark. Arguably the prettiest version of the contemporary A-body was the Skylark convertible, with its clean lines and neat profile. Grosvenor Square was a profitable stamping-ground for me, being home to not only the US Embassy, seen behind this car, but also the American Military Attache.

Plate 16   1965 Buick Wildcat. Full-size Buicks for 1965 wore all-new styling, including a dramatic W-shape at the front, with the front fenders angling forward where they encompassed the headlamps. The mid-price Wildcat had retained its sporting pretensions, with a distinctive grille and side trim which incorporated dummy vents; the two-door hardtop had a sweeping semi-fastback silhouette to its roofline.

Plate 17   **1965 Buick Wildcat.** The soft-top version of the '65 Wildcat was just as appealing to the eye as its steel-roofed contemporaries – this one seen in a backstreet between Park Lane and North Audley Street.

Plate 18   **1965 Buick Riviera.** The Riviera had seen little change for 1964, at least in styling terms, but for 1965 the stylists saw fit to hide the headlamps behind the front-fender grilles which had up to now housed the parking and turn-signal lights. The result was an unfortunate shift in the balanced appearance of the car, making it look taller and more bulky – sales, however, remained strong.

Plate 19   1966 Buick Electra 225. The '66 full-size Buicks again carried over the previous year's bodyshells; this Electra shows off the new grille, with its more prominent central portion, and the reframed headlamps. This one tried to sneak past me on Piccadilly – but I was ready for it!

Plate 20   1966 Buick Skylark. Throughout this period, GM alternated new platforms between the full-size and intermediate models, so 1966 saw all-new A-body cars. Styling followed the previous theme, but more emphatic rear-fender humps mark this as the new '66 Skylark, along with the W-shaped front borrowed from the contemporary full-sized cars.

Plate 21   1966 Buick Wildcat. Carrying over the 1965 body shell, the 1966 Wildcat had styling somewhat simplified, with its cleaner grille and neater rear end. This four-door hardtop managed to keep something of the sleekness of the two-door model despite its necessarily more upright roofline.

Plate 22   1966 Buick Riviera. The Riviera received a new body for 1966, which was shared with Oldsmobile's new Toronado. The new styling was very striking, continuing the razor-edge elements of the old shell and combining them with the sharp, angular frontal appearance seen here. The buyers liked it – sales jumped by ten thousand.

Plate 23   1967 Buick Wildcat. Swooping side creases in the new 1967 body carried a distant echo of Buick's once-famous style of side mouldings from the early fifties, and, combined with the sharp, taut lines kept the distinctive appeal of the full-size Buick. London's major hotels often did me proud – this is in the parking bay outside the Intercontinental.

Plate 24   1967 Buick Electra 225. The C-bodied Electra carried the same distinctive lines, with the now-traditional squared-off stern and full-width rear lights. Buick had always been a popular (relatively!) marque with British buyers, even from before the second world war, and still seemed to hold some favour through the 1960's.

Plate 25   1969 Buick Riviera. By now, the new-for-1966 Riviera was beginning to show its age, the body looking unfortunately heavy after its third restyling, although the appeal of the package was undiminished. In the 1960's you would usually find American cars, as here, parked anywhere in the myriad streets of the West End.

Plate 26   1970 Buick Electra 225. Another embassy to use Buicks in London was that of Kuwait – this was their brand-new carriage, spotted outside the Intercontinental Hotel at the Southern end of Park Lane, on what must have been one of my last forays into the Nation's Capital.

Plates 27 & 27a   **1953 Cadillac 62 Series.** Cadillac, like Buick, had always enjoyed a certain following among Britain's luxury-car buyers from pre-war days, lasting on through the fifties and sixties – as long as they were readily obtainable, in fact. The 62 series was the 'regular' model line – insofar as there was a cheap Cadillac, this was it! The 62 Series four-door sedan outsold all other models by a very large margin in the early 1950's, only succumbing with the growing popularity of the pillarless models as the decade progressed.

Plate 28   **1954 Cadillac 62 Series.** A new body shell for 1954 showed the gradual straightening and smoothing of lines which was the name of the game through the fifties; and Cadillac's kicked-up rear fender, originally styled after the Lockheed Lightning fighter, became more emphatic. This grubby '54 was cruising the King's Road in Chelsea when I grabbed its picture.

Plate 29   **1955 Cadillac 62 Series.** I have already mentioned the proliferation of nice cars I found, over the years, outside London's hotels: This immaculate Swiss-registered convertible was in front of the Grosvenor House, on Park Lane. 1955 was the last year of the 331 cubic inch V-8 first introduced in 1949 – from the mid-fifties, the horsepower race was on, and with it, the ever-growing size of the V-8 which only halted with the fuel crisis on the early seventies.

Plate 30 **1956 Cadillac Eldorado Seville.** Much less well known than the Eldorado Convertibles, the hardtop version was only produced for five years, beginning with the 1956 models. They shared all the soft-top's distinctive features, including the sharp fins and low-mounted taillights seen here, along with the higher-output engine. I came across this rarity cramped into a used-car lot somewhere out near Barking, where my sister lived at that time.

Plate 31 **1956 Cadillac 62 Series.** This '56 convertible got to be something of an old friend – I used to see it quite regularly, often around the Pall Mall and Trafalgar Square area. The paint was dull, but it was straight, clean and solid; I wonder where it is now?

Plate 32   1957 Cadillac 62 Series. Cadillac's new styling for 1957 saw the regular models acquire a version of the Eldorado's high-finned rear end, with the taillights removed to a position just above the bumper – the craze for fins was by now well under way! Cadillac always seemed to sell a larger proportion of convertibles in the UK than other manufacturers – this very smart '57 was lurking at the back of a car park, just where, I no longer remember.

Plate 33   1957 Cadillac Fleetwood 60 Special. The Fleetwood 60 was Cadillac's high-price sedan, many of which were sold into semi-formal use. It rode its own special chassis, with a four-inch-longer wheelbase than the 62 Series or Eldorado, and came equipped as standard with pretty well all the available options, and with its own distinctive interior trim and exterior mouldings. For the first time, the '57 model used a pillarless body – previous 60 Specials had been pillar sedans.

Plate 34 **1958 Cadillac 62 Series.** The restyling for '58 incorporated the paired headlights which had now become permissible under federal regulations, and fins were climbing towards their eventual peak.

Plate 35 **1958 Cadillac Eldorado Biarritz.** During the lifetime of the hardtop Eldorados, the convertible version carried the added name of Biarritz, to distinguish it from the fixed-head Seville. This '58, which I found parked on Whitehall, not far from the Admiralty, shows the shark-finned rear employed on both '57 and '58 models.

Plates 36 & 36A **1958 Cadillac Fleetwood 60.** The '58 Fleetwood 60 Special has to have carried the greatest weight of Chromium plating ever used on a car! This glittering black example was parked in a residential backstreet somewhere in Kensington.

Plate 37   1959 Cadillac 62 Series. You might argue that the '59 Cadillac was the car that did more harm to the reputation of the American car in British eyes than any other. Even now, if a newspaper editor or TV producer wants to poke fun at the admitted excesses of the US motor industry, they always pick the '59 Caddy. At the time, however, it didn't seem to have that effect – I can remember quite a number of them roaming the English highways during the sixties. This convertible was purring along Knightsbridge when I pressed the shutter.

Plate 38   1960 Cadillac Coupe de Ville. Previously, the de Ville models had been regarded as a trim option of the 62 Series cars, but from 1960, they became a separate line, available as a two-door Coupe, or four or six window Sedans, all of course pillarless. This pretty pale yellow Coupe de Ville was parked in Hertford Street, near the London Hilton.

Plate 39   **1960 Cadillac Sedan de Ville.** Six-window Sedan models used this conventional roofline, with small rear quarterlights being the 'sixth' windows – four-window cars had the notorious flat-top roof, with its spectacular wrap-around rear window. Only the formal long-wheelbase 75 Series cars now had fixed window pillars.

Plate 40   **1960 Cadillac Fleetwood 60.** The Fleetwood 60 Special remained Cadillac's top-price sedan, although it now rode the same wheelbase as the 62 Series and de Ville sedans. As before, most options came as standard, and distinctive exterior trim marked it out from the regular models. The River Thames at Victoria Embankment makes an attractive backdrop to this picture.

Plate 41   1961 Cadillac 62 Series. With the fins now diminishing, for '61 Cadillac added a new dimension – a fin along the lower body. The new bodyshell had a much cleaner, lighter look, exemplified by this regular-model convertible.

Plate 42   1961 Cadillac Fleetwood 60. A new touch for the 60 Special Sedan was its own, distinctive roofline, giving it a rather more formal air than the regular sedans. The dummy louvres, once a 60 Series trademark, returned, to be placed in the angle of the rear pillar. This car was, again, one I came to know quite well – although I never did figure out the significance of the registration letters CUW.

Plate 43   1962 Cadillac Sedan de Ville. The pillarless sedans still came in a choice of four or six window – this is the four-window, the six-window as before had a small rear quarter window and a thinner c-pillar. '62 styling simply 'tidied up' the '61 shell.

Plate 44   1962 Cadillac Eldorado Biarritz. Even though the Seville hardtop model was now dead, the Biarritz name remained attached to the Eldo convertible. By now, the distinctive styling of the earlier cars had also vanished, only a unique style of exterior moulding distinguishing the Eldorado from the regular convertible. This car was often parked outside the nightclub then hosted by George Raft, in Berkeley Square – I used to wonder if it might have been his car. Wishful thinking, probably!

Plate 45   1962 Cadillac Fleetwood 60. The semi-formal roofline, with its razor-edge crease over the rear window, was to stay with the 60 Special for a number of years. This smart gold car was about six years old when I photographed it, I think in a turning off of Piccadilly.

Plate 46   1962 Cadillac Fleetwood 75. The 75 Series had for many years been Cadillac's long-chassis model, listed as a formal sedan or limousine. At this time, you could also still buy a bare chassis, and have coachbuilt bodywork fitted – although funeral directors were pretty well the only takers now, along with hospitals. A number of London Embassies used Cadillacs, but most seem to have opted for the handier Fleetwood 60 sedan rather than the more bulky 75 Limousine.

Plate 47 **1963 Cadillac Sedan de Ville.** For just two years, Cadillac offered a special Sedan de Ville, appropriately enough for city use, called the Park Avenue. The '62 and '63 Park Avenue Sedans were identical with the normal sedans, except for having a shorter trunk, reducing the overall length by around eight inches. This oddball used to live at an apartment block in Addison Road, near Earls Court.

Plate 48 **1963 Cadillac Fleetwood 60.** Caught on Piccadilly, where it runs to the North of Green Park, this '63 60 Special seems to have suffered some damage to the grille. The 1963 restyling gave Cadillac a somewhat heavier look than the previous models.

Plate 49 **1964 Cadillac 62 Series.** '64 models were a face-lift of the '63s, and saw the famous Caddy fins reduced still further. The new, simpler grille gave the front a lighter, less complex feel with its less-generous use of bright metal trim.

Plate 50 **1965 Cadillac de Ville.** '65 saw something of a rethink of the Cadillac line-up: The old 62 Series was gone, to be replaced by the Calais, and the low-price convertible, seen here, became part of the de Ville series; and all sedans were four-window styles, with the rear quarterlight consigned to the stylist's dustbin. The all-new body for '65 was quite radical in its own way, with its clean, straight lines, vertically-paired headlights and tidy if cavernous cross-hatch grille.

Plate 51   1965 Cadillac Fleetwood. The Fleetwood 60 Special, though still available, was no longer the prestige model; a new Fleetwood Brougham topped it in terms of equipment, and came as standard with the padded vinyl roof covering which distinguished it. I shot this Brougham in Conduit Street, home, ironically perhaps, of the Rolls-Royce showroom.

Plate 52   1965 Cadillac Fleetwood Eldorado. Yes, that's right, the Eldorado was now regarded as a part of the Fleetwood line. Its exterior trim reflected that of the Fleetwood sedans, as did its level of equipment – any sporting pretensions were long gone. This one was captured by a little arcade of shops, yards along Park Lane from the Hilton Hotel.

Plate 53   1965 Cadillac Fleetwood 75. No, I haven't made a mistake – it was an unexplained anomaly of production that the 75 series for 1965 continued the styling of the '64 models. Using its own platform, the new version of the 75 didn't appear until the '66 model year; the '65 carried on with a platform which actually dated back to 1959, as is evident if you look carefully at the windscreen shape.

Plate 54   1966 Cadillac Calais. '66's restyle of the '65 body reduced the amount of bright metal, but at the same time brought back a rather complex grille. This was an example of the new low-price line, replacing the old 62 Series.

Plate 55   1967 Cadillac de Ville. Another two years meant another new bodyshell. The mid-sixties fashion for straight-lined razor-edge shapes came to something of a pinnacle with the '67 Cadillac – I found this convertible in a road called Pitts Head Mews, near the Hilton again, which always sounded to me as if it should have been in a Yorkshire mining village.

Plate 56   1967 Cadillac Fleetwood. The Fleetwood Brougham continued as the top-price sedan model – this one photographed from my favourite spot in Park Lane, by the one-way circuit at the corner of Hyde Park.

Plate 57   1967 Cadillac Eldorado. The Eldorado name graced an all-new car for '67. The front-wheel-drive Oldsmobile Toronado (see Plate 218) had appeared for 1966, using the same basic shell as Buick's restyled Riviera, and for '67 Cadillac got its own version of this ground-breaking design, mating the 429-cid Cadillac engine with the front-drive TH 425 transmission in the same platform. The new Eldorado got its own distinctive and elegant styling, as seen here, with concealed headlights appearing for the first time on a Caddy.

Plate 58   1969 Cadillac Fleetwood. '69 saw a return to a more conservative style, as evidenced by this Fleetwood Brougham, spotted in one corner of Grosvenor Square. Engines had now reached 472 cubic inches, only to be surpassed, a few years later, by Cadillac's own gargantuan 500-cid unit.

Plate 59 **1956 Chevrolet Bel Air.** I used to spend a lot of time wandering the backstreets of Belgravia, Chelsea and Kensington – and sometimes turned up real rarity. One such expedition revealed this rather sad-looking '56 Nomad. A year or two later, I paid £30 for a '56 Bel Air hardtop – what would we give for either one now?

Plate 60 **1958 Chevrolet Impala.** I used to travel from Oxford to London by coach, arriving at Victoria Coach Station. This '58 Impala convertible was my first discovery on one such trip – literally in the street just around the corner from the arrival bays, in Buckingham Palace Road.

Plate 61   1958 Chevrolet Impala. The Impala was a new intro for '58, with some sporting aspirations, available only as a two-door hardtop or convertible; the full line only appeared the next year. This hardtop, captured outside the American Embassy, shows off the Impala's special exterior trim very nicely.

Plate 62   1959 Chevrolet Impala. Now with of a full line-up of body types, the '59 Impala shared GM's spectacular approach to styling for that year. This enthusiastically-driven convertible was heading North on Park Lane when I spotted it, just by the turn that leads into Hyde Park on the South Carriage Drive.

Plate 63   1962 Chevrolet Bel Air. Bel Air was now the mid-price Chevrolet line, the two-door sedan its cheapest body style. Chevrolets were so numerous around my home town then, that I only rarely bothered to photograph them in London – Chevy fans will prefer some of the later editions of these books, I suspect, when I will focus on the cars I captured around Oxford!

Plate 64   1962 Chevrolet Corvair. Corvair was GM's first entry in the compact-car slot, first introduced for 1960. Leaning heavily on the technology of its perceived rival, the VW Beetle, it used a rear-mounted air-cooled engine in a surprisingly smart and distinctive body. Never perhaps the success that Chevrolet might have hoped, it remained a Chevy exclusive until its demise in 1969. This is the '62 version; a mid-priced Corvair 700 sedan.

Plate 65   1963 Chevrolet Impala SS. Having expanded the Impala to a full line in 1959, Chevrolet tried another leap onto the sporty bandwagon in 1962 with the Impala SS. Once again only available as hardtop or convertible, with distinctive trim outside and in, this smart '63 example was caught parked on Piccadilly, along the Western part where it runs along the side of Green Park.

Plate 66   1964 Chevrolet Biscayne. Opposite end of the full-size Chevy price span was the Biscayne. Favoured by such as US government agencies and taxi companies, this unusual right-hand-drive Biscayne would seem from its registration number to have been some kind of official carriage.

Plate 67   1964 Chevrolet Chevelle Malibu. After the Corvair, Chevrolet tried several more assaults on the compact market. The conventionally-engineered Chevy II (see plate 74) arrived in 1962; with the new up-sized A-body Buick Special, Olds F-85 and Pontiac Tempest in 1964, Chevy also got their own version of this shell in the form of the intermediate Chevelle. Malibu was the top-price model; this is the sporty version, a Malibu SS convertible.

Plate 68   1964 Chevrolet Corvair Monza. Top-price Corvair was the Monza 900 – mid-1962 saw the arrival of a really hot version, in the Monza Spyder. Powered by a turbocharged flat six engine, the Spyder could only be bought as a hardtop or convertible – turbocharging appeared at the same time on the Olds F-85 Jetfire, fitted to the 215-cid alloy V-8, making these the world's first turbocharged production cars.

Plate 69   **1965 Chevrolet Chevelle.** A neat restyling updated the Chevelle for '65. This is the Malibu Station Wagon, an export car in the showroom of London's GM dealer, Lendrum and Hartmann, not long after their move into new and very plush premises in Flood Street, Chelsea, and, as can be seen from the background, before they had really settled in.

Plate 70   **1965 Chevrolet Chevelle.** The clean, even elegant, lines of the Malibu two-door hardtop are evident in this street-side shot. With Chevelle, Chevrolet division at last had a really successful smaller car on their hands.

Plate 71   1965 Chevrolet Biscayne. Another right-hand-drive car, the 'Canada' legend on the number plate gives a clue to the usage of this Biscayne; the number itself suggests a possible military application, being similar to British military registrations.

Plate 72   1965 Chevrolet Impala. Two-door hardtop models of the new GM B-body for 1965 all shared these graceful semi-fastback lines, which worked particularly well on the Chevrolet sheet-metal. This Impala two-door was driving along Eccleston Street, on my walking route from Victoria Coach Station to the West End, one day just after I had arrived in the Capital.

Plate 73   1965 Chevrolet Impala. Carrying a 1964 registration number (this was in the days when the suffix letter still changed on January 1st), this RHD Impala convertible was probably the last picture I took in the old Lendrum and Hartmann showroom, in an old block in Albemarle Street, a turning off of Piccadilly. Cars were displayed on several floors, presumably raised and lowered in a suitable-sized lift, with the main showroom, seen here, on the ground floor.

Plate 74   1966 Chevrolet Chevy II. With the lack of success of the Corvair, the Chevy II was a conventional compact added to the line in 1962. Restyled for 1966, this is the lowest-priced Chevy II 100 Station Wagon, spotted outside the US Embassy in Grosvenor Square.

Plate 75   **1966 Chevrolet Impala.** Opposite end of Chevrolet's price-span for '66, this Impala hardtop shows the clean restyle of the sleek B-body models for their second year.

Plate 76   **1967 Chevrolet Chevelle.** The GM A-body saw its second-generation shell appear for 1966 – the '67 version of the Chevelle took on this rather angular look. This Malibu four-door hardtop was making a rapid circuit of the one-way system at Hyde Park Corner, turning from Duke of Wellington Place into Grosvenor Place as I fired the shutter.

Plate 77   **!967 Chevrolet Impala.** Alternating with the A-body, GM's B-body full-size cars were all-new for '67. The new Chevrolet had this rather more aggressive frontal styling, well displayed by an Impala Station Wagon.

Plate 78   **1967 Chevrolet Impala.** Emphatic hips were all the rage in the mid-sixties – the play of light on the side panels of this Impala four-door shows off Chevrolet's interpretation of this style admirably. I think this picture was taken in Cavendish Square – but I have to admit being no longer certain!

Plate 79   **1967 Chevrolet Camaro.** Never ones to let a good idea pass them by, Chevrolet responded to the success of Ford's Mustang, a few years later, with the Camaro. Introduced for 1967, the Chevy pony-car entry came as a hardtop or convertible – this is a brand-new base-line hardtop, pictured in Lendrum and Hartmann's showroom.

Plate 80   **1967 Chevrolet Camaro.** The RS was a special package available on Camaros, which included distinctive exterior details like the concealed headlights seen on this hardtop, also in the L&H showroom, on the same occasion as the last picture.

Plate 81   **1967 Chevrolet Camaro.** The soft-top version of the new Camaro, neatly parked on a yellow line! But perhaps the New York plate excuses the owner, if he maybe did not understand our parking laws.

Plate 82   **1968 Chevrolet Chevelle.** A new and very curvaceous bodyshell graced the '68 GM A-body intermediates. Chevrolet's version was an aggressive-looking beast, especially in this Malibu SS convertible guise.

Plate 83 **1968 Chevrolet Impala.** The '68 reworking of Chevrolet's full-size cars made them look somehow bigger than the '67 models, the more complicated grille and bumper adding to this effect. This Impala Sedan was pictured on the same day as the Canadian Embassy's Lincoln (see Plates 181/A), and just around the corner in Grosvenor Square; the CD plate and registration might suggest a possible link!

Plate 85 **1959 Chevrolet Corvette.** In 1958, the Vette acquired the newly-legal paired headlights, giving it a more aggressive frontal appearance. This '59 model, missing a few of the vertical plates from its grille, had belonged to Diana Dors – hence the registration number. I'm told the number 47 had a certain significance in regard to the good lady's figure. [Not in date order - the 1957 model follows on next page].

Plates 84 & 84A   **1957 Chevrolet Corvette.**   Spotted one evening as I traversed the city on my journey from Oxford to Ware, in Hertfordshire, where I was then working, this delightful '57 Vette was parked in Chester Square. The date would have been around mid-1966, I think – the car was an unusual shade of metallic blue, with silver side coves. I am sure that no-one reading this book needs to be told the history of America's only true sports car!

Plate 86   1964 Chevrolet Corvette. The Sting Ray Corvette saw production first for 1963 – based on the Sting Ray show car of the previous year, the all-new chassis and beautiful fibreglass body made it real contender against the rest of the world's sports cars. Details changes only were made for 1964, and indeed for the duration of the first-generation Sting Ray's life, which lasted until the '67 model year. In the picture, a '64 roadster hustles down Park Lane in the sunshine.

Plate 87   1965 Chevrolet Corvette. A '65 Sting Ray roadster, top up this time, taken in almost exactly the same spot as the last picture. Note the different wheels, and altered vents behind the front wheel arch – these were now effective, extracting air from the underhood region and around the front brakes.

Plate 88   1966 Chevrolet Corvette. Looking at this sequence, Park Lane must have been a favoured route among Vette owners! This '66 hardtop was caught a little further North, somewhere around the area of the Grosvenor House Hotel. Most noticeable exterior change for '66 was the cross-hatch grille.

Plate 89   1954 Chrysler New Yorker. Actually a top-of-the-line New Yorker de Luxe, this pristine-looking sedan was one of the first Chryslers to show the styling influence of Virgil Exner. His update of the rather stolid old bodyshell for '54 presaged the total redesign of all the Corporation's cars for 1955. Exner had worked with Raymond Loewy on the radical '53 Studebaker, only to be head-hunted by Chrysler to drag them out of the styling doldrums they seemed to have slipped into in the early fifties.

Plate 90   **1955 Chrysler Windsor.** Displaying the up-to-the-minute clean lines of Exner's new style, this low-price Windsor sedan, carrying a French registration, was cruising Park Lane when I spotted it. At this time, Windsors still came with the 264-cid straight six engine – the New Yorker's 331 V-8 was optional.

Plate 91   **1956 Chrysler New Yorker.** A two-door St Regis hardtop coupe, in red, white and black, made a spectacular sight in 1956 – and no less so, ten years or so later, when I photographed this one. The '56 restyle saw higher fins, following the fashion of the time; all of Virgil Exner's styling had a fluidity of line which set it apart from the crowd.

Plates 92 & 92A   **1957 Chrysler 300C.** The first 300, introduced in 1955, was so called for the fairly obvious reason of its 300 brake horsepower, the first production car to boast such an output. By 1957, this was up to 375, with 390 available optionally, from the 392-cid hemi, and you could have a convertible, as well, although they are extremely rare! '57 styling was again all-new, with the now-famous 'dart' lines, giving the Chrysler a superbly clean, elegant shape when you put it up against, say, a '57 Mercury or '57 Pontiac.

Plates 93 & 93A **1960 Chrysler New Yorker.** 1960 saw another complete restyle from Exner's pen, and the change to a unit body form of construction across the line, except for the Imperial. The old hemi V-8s had gone after 1958, to be replaced by the RB series of big-block engines in 383 and 413 cubic inch displacements; New Yorker's 413 put out 345 bhp, making this convertible itself no slouch on the highway.

Plate 94   1960 Chrysler 300F. The 300 was still going in 1960, the optional engine, a 413, now hitting the dizzying heights of 400 bhp. All the initialled-300 cars came with stiffer suspension, up-rated brakes as well as the high-output engines; for '60, you could order a four-speed manual gearbox – though not many buyers did! A backdrop which must be getting familiar by now – Park Lane, with Hyde Park in the background.

Plate 96   1964 Chrysler 300. In what might be seen as a silly move, Chrysler diluted the impact of the 300-letter cars by renaming the mid-price line as the 300 (no letter!), in 1962. These poor-man's 300s picked up many of the styling touches of their big brother's in a much cheaper and less sporting package, and led, at the company's own admission, to the demise of the initialled 300 after 1965. This four-door '64 car was found parked outside the Royal Albert Hall, no less! [Not in date order - the 1963 model follows on next page].

Plate 95 & 95A   1963 Chrysler 300J. Considering the rarity of 300-letter cars, I seem to have done exceptionally well for them! Only 400 of these '63 hardtops were produced, and for that one year, the convertible was dropped, only to be re-introduced for '64. The tail-down pose of this car, taking off from the traffic lights crossing Park Lane in the autumn of 1964, gives perhaps an impression of the urge of that big 413. Interiors, like Ford's Thunderbird, had four bucket seats rather than the benches usual at the time.

Plate 97 **1964 Chrysler 300.** The two-door hardtop was much the prettier, with its flying-bridge roof trim and part-vinyl roof. The neat square stern of the '64 is evident on this example, parked at the rear of the US Embassy in Grosvenor Square.

Plate 98 **1965 Chrysler Newport.** Newport replaced Windsor as the low-price Chrysler in 1961. This '65 Station Wagon, with its French number plates, became an old friend – I would often find it parked in Portland Place, near the BBC's Broadcasting House, but captured this shot of it driving somewhere, I no longer remember just where, in the West End.

Plate 99 **1965 Chrysler New Yorker.** Still king of the hill, price-wise, in the Chrysler line-up for 1965 was the New Yorker. This fully-equipped two-door hardtop shows of the unique glass-enclosed headlights which sparked something of a debate in US automotive circles. Virgil Exner had departed in 1961, but it was not until 1965 that the last of his influence had vanished from the Corporation's styling; his replacement as chief stylist was Elwood P. Engle, poached from Ford's Lincoln Division.

Plate 100 **1966 Chrysler Newport.** Engle's conventional but very pretty '65 Chrysler acquired a slightly squarer look for 1966, particularly at the front end. Why the owner of this striking Newport Station Wagon felt the need for those extravagant air-horns on the front fender I'll never understand!

61

Plate 101   1966 Chrysler 300. With the previous year's 300L the last of the letter-300 series, the regular 300 had to carry all of Chrysler's sporting aspirations for '66; although, with the Mustang now on the scene, smaller cars were seen as the way to go in this sphere now. The controversial glass-covered headlights were gone from all but the Imperial after just one year, and the '66 300's grille was thrustingly aggressive.

Plate 102   1967 Chrysler Newport. Base-level Chryslers had always gained a certain favour among military officialdom – this gleaming black sedan, carrying its badge of rank, was parked by the US naval attache's establishment in Grosvenor Square.

Plate 103   1967 Chrysler New Yorker. The new sculptured, angular body for '67 somehow looked better on the cheaper Chryslers – this New Yorker has a very fussy look around the front end, although the rear was somewhat neater. Probably a visitor to the Hilton, this one was parked again in Pitts Head Mews, just around the corner.

Plate 104   1968 Chrysler New Yorker. Another hotel resident, this four-door hardtop was parked in front of the Grosvenor House. A restyle of the front end resulted in this much more satisfactory look for the '68 model – engines for the 300 and New Yorker had gone up to 440 cubic inches in 1966, and stayed there until the fuel crisis of the early seventies.

Plate 105   1955 De Soto Diplomat. Chrysler Corporation were past masters of badge engineering, especially when it came to export cars. The De Soto Diplomat, built exclusively for export, was always in fact just a Plymouth under the skin, although some years a 'real' De Soto front clip was fitted to the body. This '55, however, only has a distinctive toothy grille to set it apart from its more mundane brethren.

Plate 106   1958 De Soto Diplomat. From '57 until '59, Diplomats gained the front-end sheet metal of a genuine De Soto, although the distinctively Plymouth fin shape gives them away very easily. This Diplomat Custom was captured while waiting at traffic lights by the A4 in Brentford.

Plate 107   1953 Dodge Coronet. In 1953, Dodge too gained a V-8 – a little 241-cid unit. The hood motif on this Coronet Eight gives you the clue – and note also the rams-head ornament. This tidy example, spotted in a backstreet somewhere around Hammersmith, shows the rather dumpy styling which earmarked Chrysler products in pre-Exner days.

Plate 108   1954 Dodge Coronet. Exner's influence first appeared with this much-improved version of the old bodyshell – the more stylish grille, hooded headlights – and note here the stylised rams-head. English car collectors might notice the odd Morris Eight roadster parked behind the Dodge.

Plate 109   **1955 Dodge Royal.** The Royal nameplate had appeared for '54, and became a full line for '55. This sedan, pictured in the familiar surroundings of Park Lane, shows off the new, sleek body, and the distinctive cutaway style of the taillights which would be a Dodge feature for the next few years.

Plate 110   **1956 Dodge Custom Royal.** Ever searching for a better clientele, the Custom Royal became the top-price Dodge from '55; and the V-8 had gone up to 270 cubic inches in '55, then to 315 for '56, with the first of the D-500 performance option cars available. This very clean (restored, even at ten years old?) convertible has a slightly non-original paint job – the hood should match the front fenders!

Plate 111 **1957 Dodge Coronet.** By now, Coronet was Dodge's lowest-priced car. The new Forward-Look bodyshell for '57 looks well on this convertible, which I actually photographed from the front seat of a bus, somewhere in Edmonton, near the North Circular Road. Base engine in Coronet was still the old flathead 230-cid straight six, with the 325 V-8 optional.

Plate 112 **1959 Dodge Custom Royal.** Dodge's developing version of the Forward Look reached its pinnacle in '59, with this dramatic styling. This sedan, with its rather understated grey and black colour scheme, was parked in the centre of Regent Street.

Plate 113   1960 Dodge Dart Pioneer. A revised line-up appeared for 1960, with a cheaper Dart line priced below the Matador and Polara models; this is the Dart Pioneer, middle of the low-price line. This black sedan was Trans-World Airlines London courtesy car – I found its numberplate, TWA 1, on a 1966 Ford Galaxie some years later; presumably its replacement in the fleet.

Plate 114   1961 Dodge Polara. Official car of the Sudanese Embassy, SUD 1 is an example of the 'big' full-size Dodge for '61, riding on a 122 inch wheelbase. Darts used a shorter 118 inch platform, and new for '61 was Dodge's compact Lancer line. New styling remained as quirky as ever, with the unique 'wrong way round' fins curling around the inset tubular taillights.

Plate 115   1961 Dodge Dart Phoenix. The '61 Dart used different rear styling, with taillights set just above the bumper – if the grille looks vaguely familiar, consider the Mark III Ford Zodiac of two years later…! Engine choices in the Darts began with the new-for-1960 slant six, or a full line of V-8's.

Plate 116   1962 Dodge Dart 440. Dodge changed to suffix numbers to distinguish the series in '62. The restyled Darts were 330's or 440's, with a new sporty Polara 500, based on the same short wheelbase, at the top of the line-up. The 'big' Dodge was gone, only to reappear in mid-year as the Custom 880, based on the Chrysler platform.

Plate 117   1963 Dodge Dart GT. Just to confuse everyone, in '63 Dodge relabelled their compact car as the Dart – this was the top-of-the-line sporty version. 'Small' full-sized cars were now just 330 or 440, with the 'big' Custom 880 heading things up.

Plate 118   1963 Dodge Polara 500. Top of the 'small' cars was still the sporty Polara. Even in '63, styling still showed the flamboyance of Virgil Exner's influence – this convertible, with its missing headlight trim, was parked in New Bond Street. Polaras came as standard with the 318 small-block V-8, with the bigger B-blocks optional.

Plate 119   **1964 Dodge 440.** Styling for '64 was toned down under Engle's guidance, leaving the 440 with this clean, distinctive appearance – station wagons like this had a particularly interesting shape with their long, sleek rooflines.

Plate 120   **1964 Dodge 440.** Looking slightly lost as they cruised around Piccadilly Circus, this Swiss family had the relatively unusual two-door sedan, very smart in its polished black paintwork. Engine choices remained as before, from the slant six up to a 383-cid V-8; for serious tyre-burners, the 426 Hemi could be bought off the showroom floor in a sedan like this one…!

Plate 121   1964 Dodge Dart GT. Dodge's compact Dart changed little for '64, as this GT hardtop, shot in the pouring rain, shows, although mid-year saw the Dart get its own optional V-8 power with the appearance of the new 273 cubic inch version of the small-block engine.

Plate 122   1965 Dodge Polara. All changed again for '65: The Dart went on pretty much as before, but the 'small' full-size car shrank by two inches in wheelbase to become officially an intermediate, using the revived Coronet name. An all-new full-size line-up now carried the Polara and Custom 880 nameplates, although, in another apparent attempt to keep us confused, export cars were labelled as 'Polara 880'. This wagon, however, is a genuine US-market Polara – missing part of the street name should read Upper Brook Street.

Plate 123   1965 Dodge Custom 880. This, also genuine US, wagon shows off its optional wood-grain side trim. A new top-of-the-line Monaco was available only as a two-door hardtop for '65, to be expanded to a full series for '66.

Plate 124   1965 Dodge Polara 880. The export-only Polara 880 had the same level of interior trim as the regular Polara, but came, for the UK Market, in right-hand-drive form, as seen here. Standard export engine was the small-block 318 V-8.

Plate 125 & 125A   1966 Dodge Charger. By the mid-sixties, the sports/ponycar boom was well under way. Not just the small Mustang and its clones, but the intermediate-size platforms were spawning a new breed of performance-optioned models, among which the fastback was becoming the preferred style – Chrysler Corp.'s entry here was the Charger, based on the Dodge Coronet. The radical roofline, full-width taillight and retractable headlights set it apart from regular Coronets; heavy-duty suspension gave it agile roadholding, and engine choices from the 318 up to a 383-4V provided the urge – in 1967, the 426 hemi was added to the option list in an otherwise unchanged vehicle.

Plate 126 **1966 Dodge Coronet.** This Coronet 440 sedan provides a contrast with the previous plates, showing the intermediate bodyshell in its standard form. Another foreign visitor, on Austrian plates, it looks as though its owner has been misjudging narrow gaps, from the damage to the side body moulding!

Plate 127 **1966 Dodge Polara 880.** 1966's version of the export-special full-size Dodge, the Polara 880 was again a regular Polara except for its nameplates, and the right-hand-drive arrangement for markets where it was required. The fine grille texture picks up the theme of the Charger's.

Plate 128   1966 Dodge Monaco 500. With Monaco now a full line, the top-price two-door hardtop had to be elevated to a higher plane with the added '500' designation, and set apart visually by its simple body trim, with the three dummy vents behind the front wheel, and fancy wheel covers. Interiors were of the four-bucket-seat arrangement.

Plate 129   1966 Dodge Dart GT. '66 was the last year for the clean and simple bodyshell designed by Elwood Engle for the compact Dart/Valiant models. Contradictorily, this French-registered convertible is parked outside the US Embassy – a returning US serviceman, possibly?

Plate 130   1952 Ford Customline. Scruffy, its paintwork dull and faded, I came across this rare '52 Customline Country Sedan tucked down a narrow residential street in Earls Court during one of my annual trips to the Motor Show. Popular Ford engine then was the ubiquitous flathead V-8, although a straight six had been added as long ago as 1941.

Plate 131   1958 Ford Fairlane 500. Perhaps it is an indication of how common cars like full-size Fords were then that, on visits to London, I only bothered to photograph the very unusual. For anyone who hasn't already spotted it, this is indeed a Skyliner retractable hardtop, cruising Park Lane despite its lack of wheel covers.

Plate 132   1959 Ford Fairlane 500 Galaxie. In mid-'59, Ford introduced a new up-market model, with a formal-style roof derived from the T-Bird, as can be seen clearly in this shot of the two-door hardtop version. By taking a huge bite out of the lower-end of its price bracket, this could be called the car that killed the Edsel – a strange decision by Ford's corporate management!

Plate 133   1960 Ford Fairlane 500. In '60, Galaxies lost the Fairlane tag whilst keeping their squared-off rooflines; this two-door Fairlane 500 sedan shows the cheaper model's roof, with its huge rear window – if the rear end looks a little odd, that's because the rear bumper is a bit out of shape!

Plate 134   1962 Ford Galaxie 500. Ford were playing the name-swap game in '62 – Fairlane became the new intermediate car, smaller than a Ford but bigger than a Falcon, and as a result the full-size range had to be expanded by adding a '500' to designate the higher-priced version of the Galaxie. Fords had long been available in RHD form, usually built in Canada, which had in pre-war years led to the quaint 'Empire Made' badge which adorned the dashboards.

Plate 135   1963 Ford Falcon Futura. Ford's compact entry, arriving in 1960 as had the Chevrolet Corvair and Plymouth's Valiant, was the very-conventional Falcon, with its neat little 144-cid straight six engine. By 1963, with rather more ornate styling, the 260 cubic inch V-8 had appeared to offer a bit more urge for those who ordered it, coming as standard in the Futura Sprint.

Plate 136   1963 Ford Galaxie 500 XL. The 500 XL had first appeared in mid-62, when Ford had a sudden rush of sports-car fever, accompanying as it did the Falcon Sprint, the Fairlane 500 Sports Coupe and the T-Bird Sports Roadster. This four-door hardtop was added to the XL line-up for '63 – the spinner wheel covers and oval badge on the C-pillar give it away.

Plate 137   1964 Ford Falcon Futura Sprint. Available only as a two-door hardtop or convertible, the Sprint had the 260-cid V-8 fitted as standard – by the year's end, you could also have the Mustang's 271-horsepower hipo 289 as an option. In case anyone has forgotten, the Falcon Sprints put up an excellent showing in the Monte Carlo Rallies of '63, '64 and '65, as well as performing very well on the racing circuits of Britain for a number of years.

Plate 138   1965 Ford Fairlane 500. Sparkling in the autumn sunshine, this '65 Sports Coupe with its Arabic number plates was brand new when I captured it in late 1964. The very bluff shape of front and rear did a considerable disservice to the rather pretty '64 Fairlane bodyshell after its restyle, intended presumably to bring it into line with the all-new, very boxy '65 Galaxie.

Plate 139   1965 Ford Galaxie 500. Another example of the Canadian-assembled RHD export Fords, this Galaxie four-door hardtop was photographed from the island area of Hyde Park Corner. '65 styling underwent a sudden change from the sleek curves of previous years to this very angular appearance, which would be softened considerably in subsequent years. Export cars usually had the 289 small-block V-8 and three-speed Cruis-o-matic transmission, although other choices were available.

Plate 140   1965 Ford Galaxie 500 LTD. The 500 LTD was new for '65, a highly-equipped luxury version of the full-size Ford – this is the two-door model, pictured outside the Grosvenor House Hotel. LTD advertising caused a furore by claiming the car was quieter at speed than a Rolls-Royce – RR made all kinds of threats, but went suspiciously quiet themselves when Ford produced their test results....

Plate 141   1965 Ford Mustang. The Mustang revolution really began in April 1964, with the announcement of the first hardtop and convertible models – the fastback followed a few months later. Based on the simple Falcon platform, Mustang offered comfort and style, with performance to match if required – base engine was the 170-cid six, but options ranged up to the 271-hipo 289. Mustangs quickly became a common sight in the UK – this early fastback was spotted in a West-End residential mews.

Plate 142   1965 Ford Mustang. '64½ and '65 Mustangs were indistinguishable – this hardtop could be either. Vinyl roof coverings were an option that somehow sat awkwardly on the sporty lines – the lack of V-8 badges suggests this was a six-cylinder car: The 170 was quickly supplanted by the 200-cid as base engine.

Plate 143   1966 Ford Fairlane 500 GT. Ford went GT-mad in '66 – GT packages were offered on Falcon and Fairlane as well as Mustang that year, while Galaxie offered the 428-powered '7-Litre' option. This is the Fairlane 500 hardtop, with its GT package identified by the rocker-panel stripes.

Plate 144 **1966 Ford Mustang GT.** Mustang's GT package included the neat grille-mounted foglights as well as stripes and stiffer shocks. This convertible, photographed on the giratory part of Park Lane, has the added amber indicators below the bumper which were fitted in the UK to imported cars.

Plate 145 **1967 Ford Falcon Futura.** Falcon had acquired a new bodyshell in '66, which carried over with minor detail changes into '67. Top seller in the better-trimmed Futura series was this four-door sedan.

Plate 146   1967 Ford Fairlane 500. Fairlane, too, saw only detail changes for '67, as the revised grille of this sedan shows. This V-8 powered car (note the badge on the front fender), spotted near Piccadilly Circus, looks to be well overloaded!

Plate 147   1967 Ford Galaxie 500 XL. 500 XL was still regular 'sporty' full-size Ford in '67 – the '7-Litre' had lasted only one year. Big Fords were now looking much more svelte, with sleek curves softening the straight lines of a year or so earlier, and especially so, this semi-fastback two-door hardtop model.

Plate 148   1967 Ford Mustang GT. A well-optioned-up Mustang spotted parked in South Audley Street – the GT package again evident from the stripes and grille lights. Still using the Falcon floorpan, Mustang nonetheless had a new body for '67.

Plate 149   1967 Ford Mustang. By contrast, this '67 fastback looks to be a very basic version! The standard grille had the plain crossbar, returned after an absence for '66 except on the GT option; the new fastback body had a roofline which extended to the end of the trunk lid. Coincidence raises its head – this car and the previous one both have New Jersey plates!

Plate 150   1967 Ford Mustang GT. A '67 fastback this time, with the GT option, outside the US Embassy in Grosvenor Square.

Plate 151   1966 Shelby GT350. All right, perhaps I should have put these under 'S', but it has always seemed to me clearer to show the Shelby Mustangs with their parent cars. Carroll Shelby started building race versions of the Mustang as soon as they appeared – by '66, he was selling them in some numbers, not only to racing teams but to the public. This is his highly-tuned version of the 289-engined '66 fastback.

Plate 152   1967 Shelby GT500. Body modifications were becoming more noticeable on Carroll Shelby's uprated Mustangs by '67, as the front end of this car demonstrates. Available for the first time in '67 was the incredibly hairy GT500, with its tuned 428 big-block, alongside the 289-engined GT350.

Plate 153   1956 Ford Thunderbird. Thunderbird was Ford's first try at a sports car, introduced in '55 as a response to Chevrolet's Corvette. Based on regular Ford running gear, the first T-Birds were pretty two-seaters, as this '56 shows – changes for the second year were minimal, but the removable hardtop's portholes and standard-equipment external spare mark this as a '56.

Plate 154   1957 Ford Thunderbird. '57 saw more noticeable differences, with the two-seat T-Bird growing bigger fins, a mouthier grille and heavier bumpers. This super-clean example was pictured on Piccadilly, at the Western end opposite Green Park.

Plate 155   1960 Ford Thunderbird. The two-seat T-Bird disappeared after '57, to be replaced by a close-coupled four-seat car – sales showed the wisdom of this move, even if purists regretted the end of the two-seater. This '60 hardtop shows the continued 'squarebird' body introduced for '58 and carried over with only trim changes for three years – hardtops were now fixed, and the convertibles had disappearing tops derived from the Skyliner technology.

Plate 156   1962 Ford Thunderbird. Second generation of the four-seat T-Bird was the 'cigarbird', new for 1961. Again, only trim changes distinguish '61, '62 and '63 models – this '62 soft-top, pictured in Berkeley Square, has the square block grille and triple rear fender flash which define that year's cars.

Plate 157   1963 Ford Thunderbird. '63 T-Birds had, once again, revised grilles, shown off nicely by this hardtop, caught in traffic in Piccadilly. Also new for '63 was the sculptured swage line on the front fender and door. Only engine, since 1961, was the 300-hp Y-block 390 cubic inch V-8, although a 340-hp version, with twin four-barrel carbs, was optional.

Plate 158   1963 Ford Thunderbird Landau. Part of Ford's sudden upsurge of interest in sporty models in mid-62 had been two extra T-Birds, one of which was the Landau hardtop. Landaus came with a padded vinyl roof and the fake landau irons, and up-market interiors which featured woodgrain trim in place of the regular car's brushed aluminium. This '63 Landau reflects the evening sunshine on Hyde Park Corner.

Plate 160   1965 Ford Thunderbird Landau. '64 saw a third generation of four-place T-Birds, with the so-called 'bananabird' body; once again, detail changes only mark out the different years through to '66. '65s had the grille with the added vertical bars, and saw the first sequential rear turn signals, where triple bulbs gave rippling effect when the indicators were in use. For the sharp-eyed, yes, that is a '65 Riviera in the background – interesting, to see the two major rivals side by side in a London street! [Not in date order - 1963 model follows on next page].

Plates 159 & 159A   1963 Ford Thunderbird Sports Roadster. The other mid-62 T-Bird intro was the Sports Roadster: Roadsters featured Kelsey-Hayes wire wheels (yes, real ones!) which wouldn't fit under the rear wheel spats fitted to other models, hence the bare-knees look – their other distinguishing item was the removable fibreglass tonneau cover over the two rear seats, obvious in the top-down shot but also visible in the frontal view. The top could be retracted or erected with the tonneau in place – top down, the Roadster had something of the long-trunk lines of a pre-war classic roadster.

Plate 161   1966 Ford Thunderbird. Changes for '66 were more noticeable, with this altered grille and the blade bumper picked up from the Mustang's styling; at the rear, taillights went full-width for the first time. Although the Landau continued, the Roadster had died with the '63 model – a restyled tonneau, to suit the new body, could be had as an option, but the wire wheels were no more.

Plate 162   1967 Ford Thunderbird Landau. '67 saw another complete restyle, and in fact the end of the almost-traditional three-year cycle. The new car was bigger and heavier, and even included a four-door (!) Landau model, which proved popular for a while although sales declined over the years until it was dropped again in '71. This example was almost new when I came across it outside the Midland Bank in Piccadilly – checking up on the bank balance, perhaps?

Plates 163 & 163A **1955 Imperial.** The Imperial had Been Chrysler's most prestigious model since the 1920's, but had always been sold under the parent nameplate. It was only in the fifties that the Company decided it needed a brand name to compete directly with Cadillac and Lincoln; and so Imperial became a marque apart. No model names were used; the cars were just Imperials, except for the Crown Imperial Limousine, a factory-built long wheelbase eight-seater, although this two-door hardtop carried a Newport designation in common with other Chrysler two-doors. Engine was the little 331-cid hemi V-8.

Plate 164   1956 Imperial. '56 saw the fledgling Imperial continue as it had begun, with the addition of a pillarless four-door Southampton hardtop. Engine was up to 354 cubic inches, and this regular sedan, pictured sweeping regally around the Park Lane gyratory towards Hyde Park, shows off the stylish revamp of the '55 body. Interior trim in all Imperials was lavish, in an attempt to take the high ground from its competitors.

Plate 165   1957 Imperial. With its own version of the forward look, the '57 Imperial gained an expanded model list. The LeBaron became the top-priced four-door cars, with the Crown as a slightly cheaper line offering a two-door hardtop and convertible in addition. A base Imperial was still available, exemplified by this rather scruffy two-door spotted on Park Lane. Some '57s had only two headlights, depending upon whether their destination state permitted the use of quads at that time – for '58, federal law allowed the four-light arrangement.

Plates 166 & 166A   1961 Imperial LeBaron. The Imperial line-up had changed little by 1961, although there were no more pillar sedans after 1959. LeBaron was now a one-model, top-price car, distinguished from its cheaper brethren by the stylish semi-formal roofline illustrated here. Interior trim was a choice of the finest leathers or soft wool broadcloth, and the list of standard equipment allowed for very few options. The hemi engines were gone after '58, to be replaced by the tough and powerful 413-cid RB. This clean '61, showing off its quirky, dramatic Exner-penned styling with the exposed headlights and suspended taillights, was parked close by the Grosvenor House Hotel – believe it or not, the (original) paintwork was bright scarlet!

Plate 167   1964 Imperial LeBaron. '64 saw the departure of the Exner-inspired bodyshell which had begun life in 1957 – from 1960, Imperial was the only Chrysler passenger car still to use body-on-chassis construction. The new body, still using the old ladder-frame chassis, was the work of Elwood Engle, and clearly shows the same thinking as his Lincoln Continental of 1961, with clean straight lines outlined in bright metal. I came across this shining black '64 on my way to a visit to Lincoln Cars, on the Great West Road in Brentford; the pictures were actually taken in Boston Manor Road, which was where I left the tube train.

Plate 168   1965 Imperial Crown. A subtle restyle of the new shell gave this rather heavier look for '65, with the glass-enclosed headlights similar to other Chryslers. This Crown four-door was the cheapest, and by far the most popular, of the offerings in the mid-sixties; this one, parked in front of the Grosvenor House Hotel once again. London's more exclusive hotels often provided me with exciting catches, and perhaps the Grosvenor House was the most consistent of them all!

Plate 169   1965 Imperial LeBaron. Almost indistinguishable from a '64 from behind, this '65 LeBaron again shows the exclusive semi-formal style of the roof, with its smaller-than-usual rear windshield – the stylised dummy spare wheel was a carry-over from the Exner days, and would finally vanish after '66. Padded vinyl roof trim was optional, but had yet to become the popular item it would be in the sixties and seventies. I spotted this pale blue example in New Bond Street.

Plate 170   1966 Imperial Crown. Again a subtle restyle for '66, but greater changes were effected under the skin – the engine, still the RB block, went up to 440 cubic inches, and disc brakes made their appearance. This white Crown carries a black vinyl roof – contrast which is a photographer's nightmare! I was just talking about hotels – this is the forecourt of the Hilton, on Park Lane.

Plate 171   1967 Imperial LeBaron. '66 saw the last of the separate chassis; '67 Imperials used a common unit body platform with regular Chryslers, although styling and trim were still very much their own. This brand-new LeBaron was cruising my favourite hunting ground of Park Lane, in the sunshine of the early spring of '67.

Plate 172   1969 Imperial LeBaron. The continuing re-absorption of Imperial into the Chrysler line took another step in '69, when some sheet-metal was shared with the all-new 'fuselage-look' Chryslers. Imperial managed to remain reasonably distinctive, with exclusive front and rear treatments, but the writing was on the wall – the marque disappeared after 1975. And talking of hotels; this was shot outside one which didn't give me much success, as a rule – the Dorchester, of all places!

Plate 173   **1953 Lincoln Capri.** The car which the Imperial was supposed to compete with! Lincoln was second only to Cadillac in the luxury car stakes in the early fifties. The heavy-looking, rounded styling is typical Ford of the period, of course, but it belied a surprisingly quick, nimble car – Lincolns won the Panamericana road race several years in succession! This top-of-the-range Capri sedan was parked in a sidestreet off of Finborough Road in Earls Court, one year when I went exploring after my annual visit to the Motor Show.

Plate 175   **1960 Continental Mark V.** I've chosen to list the Continentals under L for Lincoln, for simplicity's sake – the nameplate only lasted five years as its own marque, whereas Imperial did manage twenty! Ford further complicated our lives in later years, by re-using the Marks III, IV & V labels on the Thunderbird-derived two-door cars of 1968 to 1979. This is the '60 version of a Mark V, on Italian plates, showing off the reverse-slant rear windshield with its roll-down centre section which would re-emerge on Mercurys in the sixties. Regular Lincolns had different rooflines and conventional glass. [Not in date order - the 1956 model follows on next page].

Plates 174 & 174A   Continental Mark II. Just as Chrysler were deciding to upgrade the Imperial, so Ford decided to really go for broke! The Mark II Continental, marketed without the Lincoln name attached, was an attempt to grab the ultra-exclusive luxury trade. Built on a special production line, with no expense spared on materials or details, the Mark II sold a total of 1,769 cars in two years, 1956 and '57 – not enough for Ford to break even on the deal. Engines were specially-prepared 368 cid units; sleek and timeless styling was the work of Lincoln's own team. Perhaps the saddest result of the poor sales was that we never got to see the four-door Berline, or the retractable hardtop – both had been planned!

Plates 176 & 176A   1960 Continental Mark V. Perhaps claiming the title as rarest car in this book is this Mark V Limousine. The Continental Limo and Formal Sedan were only offered for '59 and '60 – the '60 Limo saw a total of just 34 cars produced. These were the only Continentals to have a conventional roofline – even convertibles had a back-sloped rear window. I have no idea who the owner of this car might have been, but it was often parked at this spot, in Upper Brook Street, just around the corner from the American Embassy.

Plate 177   1961 Lincoln Continental. For '61, Ford finally gave up on the huge, overweight aircraft carrier which the Lincoln and Continental had become. All cars were Lincolns, and only two bodies were available – a four-door sedan, or this remarkable four-door convertible. Wheelbase was down eight inches, and the beautiful lines were the work of Elwood P. Engle, before his abrupt move to Chrysler later that year. The convertible was the only production four-door soft-top anywhere in the world, and had the only totally automatic retracting mechanism seen until Mercedes-Benz reinvented it in the 1990's; the Lincoln's was based, as might be surmised, on the Skyliner technology! And an unusual backdrop – Constitution Hill, the road which leads to the Queen's front door, at Buckingham Palace.

Plate 178   1962 Lincoln Continental. This '62 Sedan shows off the revisions to Lincoln's styling for the second year of the new-look cars. A new, lighter grille with a simpler bumper also allowed the headlights to be moved forward, getting over a criticism of the '61 cars road illumination. Engines were the 430 cubic inch unit, derived from the old Lincoln block of the fifties, with a heavy-duty Ford-o-Matic trans. The picture was taken outside the offices of Lincoln Cars, on the Great West Road in Brentford, a place I was known to frequent regularly – I hope to come across more shots from that Ford Import company's premises for later volumes; I know they're still there somewhere!

Plates 179 & 179A   1964 Lincoln Continental. For 1964, the same clean, slab-sided body was stretched four inches, giving more room in the rear seats – unfortunately, the result somehow destroyed the superb proportions of the earlier cars. Both sedan and convertible had the reverse-opening rear doors – with the pillarless design of the soft-top, this necessitated an ingenious device to avoid tearing the weatherstrips when the rear door was opened: As you press the button, or pull the interior handle, the window winds itself down four inches; close the door, and it winds up again. This was the source of much amusement to onlookers, especially children, when I owned a '66 convertible for many years! I used to see this lovely dark turquoise '64 occasionally parked here, in Adams Row, behind the Britannia Hotel which fronted onto Grosvenor Square.

Plates 181 & 181A   1968 Lincoln Continental. Just as Chrysler were giving up on the Crown Imperial, Ford decided it needed a limo in the catalogue! The Continental Limousine, like the late Crowns, was built outside, in this case by US coachbuilders Lehmann – Petersen. The first limo appeared in the '64 catalogue – this '68 example, as you might guess from the number plate, was the Canadian Embassy's formal limousine, parked here in Grosvenor Street. I met this car again in later life – it turned up, without the number plates of course, in the hands of a fellow Lincoln enthusiast in the 1980's, at a number of American Auto Club rallies.

Plate 180   1967 Lincoln Continental. In '66, a new bodyshell graced the Lincoln – squarer, with more detail in its shapes, and looking rather more massive; and a two-door hardtop was added to the line-up. Changes for '67 were almost unnoticeable – only the fine vertical lines in the grille mark this sedan as a '67 car – taillights, horizontal below the back bumper, were also altered slightly. I liked the number plate – there's no doubting the owner's name!

Plate 182   1957 Mercury Commuter. Ford never seem to have much success with higher-price cars in the UK – you may have noted the paucity of fifties Lincolns already, and now the same applies to Mercurys. This four-door pillarless wagon, with its cheerful owner, was cruising along Piccadilly when I caught it on camera; the odd, extra vertical strips on the windshield are not original, but the paintwork, I am sure, was – Pink and cream, with black around the windows and along the rear fender recess!

Plate 183   1958 Mercury Monterey. A lower priced model in Mercury's line-up, this Monterey sedan tried to sneak past me on Park Lane one day – I chose the rear view, because the front bumper was well out of shape! Styling uses the same basic body as '57, but changes made the '58 look much heavier – Monterey and Montclair used a 383-cid version of the Lincoln-block engine.

Plate 184   1959 Mercury Monterey. Another restyle for '59 had a much better result – '59 Mercs still looked pretty big, but lines were cleaner, and the spectacular pie-wedge taillights made them unmistakeable from behind. Monterey was now the cheapest Mercury available, this sedan the fastest-selling offering by a big margin. I apologise for the damage to this negative, which was the result of a processing fault, but I thought it worth including if only because of the shortage of Mercurys in this part of my collection.

Plate 185   1960 Mercury Monterey. Believe it or not, this '60 is another restyle of the old bodyshell, albeit a pretty drastic one. The clean, smooth lines were a foretaste of shapes to come, in Ford and Mercury guise, even if the old, rather odd, rooflines were retained. From '59, Montereys had used the Ford 312-cid engine, with the 383 available as an option.

Plate 186   1961 Mercury Monterey. Mercury were playing the popular name-game as the sixties opened: Mercury now rode the Ford's 120 inch wheelbase chassis, and the Montclair and Park Lane models were dropped; Monterey was now the top-priced line, with a new Meteor nameplate filling the lower echelons. Styling, using the Ford shell, echoed the themes of the '60 cars. And the backdrop to this shot must be becoming monotonous for you – sorry!

Plate 187   1962 Mercury Monterey Custom. Talking of name games… For '62, Meteor, after one year as a full-size car, became an intermediate based on Ford's Fairlane – see below! Monterey needed a stable-mate, so the priciest models were now called Monterey Custom. Styling for '62 didn't change a lot – the grille bars now curved out instead of in, and a unique tunnelled taillight design made a new use of '61's fins.

Plate 188   1962 Mercury Colony Park. Staying with a long-time Ford tradition, station wagons in the Mercury line carried separate nameplates, top of which was the Colony Park with its luxurious interiors and wood-grain exterior trim. In 1965 I left school to start work in Hertfordshire, and used to travel across London on my way there from home – this car was pictured in Cheyne Walk, off the Chelsea Embankment, one of the routes I used on foot from coach to bus.

Plate 189   1962 Mercury Meteor Custom. Following the small-car explosion of the early sixties, Mercury followed the compact Comet of 1961 with its own intermediate for '62, as mentioned above. Meteor was an up-market version of the Fairlane, also new that year, which picked up styling hints from the full-size Merc including the tunnelled taillights. Meteor was only to last two years – in '64, the Comet grew somewhat in size and price-tag, and the need for the medium-size car was gone.

Plate 190   1963 Mercury Monterey S-55. Just as Ford had had a burst of sports-car gung-ho in '62, so did Mercury, introducing mid-year the S-55 hardtop and convertible as bucket-seat versions of the Monterey. In '63, they continued, to be joined by a sleek semi-fastback hardtop in the middle of that year. This cracking '63 soft-top with its gleaming gold paintwork was parked at the side of Regent Street, in the days when you could get away with that!

Plate 191   1964 Mercury Park Lane. Name games once more – for '64, Park Lane and Montclair were back, as top- and medium-price models respectively, all based on the same 120-inch wheelbase. This sparkling black Park Lane sedan with its 'Breezeway' rear window was a regular of mine, often to be seen parked on the south side of Grosvenor Square, near the Britannia Hotel.

Plate 192   1966 Mercury Comet Cyclone. By the mid-sixties Comet had grown to intermediate size, and with the Cyclone became a serious performance car as well. Engine options were the ubiquitous 289, with variations of the Y-block 390 available – side stripes mark this as a Cyclone GT, which came with the 265hp 390 as standard.

Plate 193   1967 Mercury Cougar. Mercury, of course, had to have its own variant of the Mustang sooner or later – the Cougar, using a slightly stretched Mustang platform, appeared for '67. Only available at first as this elegant hardtop, Cougar laid more emphasis on comfort than performance, although again high-output 390's were optional. By coincidence, this car as also in Cheyne Walk, on a separate occasion from the '62 wagon above.

Plate 194   1953 Oldsmobile Super 88. Early fifties Oldsmobiles had an enviable reputation for performance – the so-called 'Rocket Eighty-Eight', a result of the easy-revving 303 cubic inch V-8 introduced for 1949. The old 303 was still there in '53, but would be enlarged the next year to 324 cid – this '53 is the relatively unusual two-door sedan version.

Plate 195   1955 Oldsmobile Super 88. '55s still had the 324 engine. This Super 88 sedan was making its desultory way along a very rainy Piccadilly one day – yes, I did even go out in the rain to look for pictures! It looks pretty straight, even if the paintwork is rather dull.

Plate 196   1956 Oldsmobile 98. The 98 was Oldsmobile's top-price line, based on the bigger C-body shell shared with Cadillac but using styling almost identical with the 88s. This slightly battered-looking '56, minus its rocket-ship hood ornament, was parked in Reeves Mews, just off Park Lane near the Grosvenor House.

Plate 197 **1958 Oldsmobile Dynamic 88.** Low-price Olds for '58 became the Dynamic 88, with the 371-cid engine first introduced for '57. Sports car enthusiasts might like to scrutinise the background of this shot – note the Bristol following the Olds, and the Aston Martin DB2 going the other way!

Plate 198 **1959 Oldsmobile 98.** Olds styling for '59 was as outrageous as any other GM product that year, as this 98 Holiday hardtop sedan, cruising around the Park Lane giratory, shows. Engines now included the 394 cubic inch V-8, standard in the 98, as well as the 371.

Plate 199   **1960 Oldsmobile Super 88.** Mid-price model in the Olds line-up, this '60 shows off the revised styling for that year, the lines now much cleaner with the neat if complicated grille, and flat 'aircraft-carrier' trunk. The two-door hardtop pictured was photographed parked in Berkeley Square.

Plate 200   **1960 Oldsmobile 98.** Rear view of this 98 Holiday Sedan shows the new flaring rear bumper, and high-set taillights, making the '60 Olds as distinctive from behind as it was from in front. Coincidence strikes again – this shot was taken in Bruton Street, literally just around the corner from the last!

Plate 201   **1961 Oldsmobile Super 88.** Oldsmobile shared the more restrained turn of styling common in GM by 1961, as this Super 88 Holiday Sedan shows. The old flat-top roof was gone, replaced by this smart squared-off style; engines only ran to two power output versions of the 394, although the aluminium-block 215 had now appeared, to power the F-85 compact.

Plate 202   **1961 Oldsmobile 98.** As always, 98 shared its styling with other full-size Oldsmobiles despite using the C-body shell. The longer wheelbase and straight lines make this gleaming black car look a block long – YU1 was the official embassy car of the London establishment of Yugoslavia, suggesting that communist-inspired anti-Americanism didn't run to motor transport!

Plate 203   1961 Oldsmobile Starfire. Olds, of course, had to join in the performance car surge of the early sixties, given their previous reputation – the Starfire, using a name which had appeared briefly in the fifties, came back for '61 as this convertible-only model, officially designated as part of the Super 88 line. Brushed aluminium side trim marked the Starfire, running along the centre of the body panels – this rather scruffy car was missing the rocker panel brightwork by the time I took its picture in the late sixties.

Plate 204   1962 Oldsmobile F-85 Cutlass. The F-85 had appeared for '61, as the Olds entry in the new compact car market, and underwent only minor restyling for '62. Engine, as mentioned above, was the alloy-block 215 cubic inch V-8 – although a common design with the Buick engine, the Olds version of the block was die-cast rather than sand-cast, and became, along with Chevrolet's flat six, the first production turbocharged passenger-car engines in the world.

Plate 205   1963 Oldsmobile Starfire. From '62, Starfire had gained a two-door hardtop alongside the convertible, and became a model in its own right. This '63 shows off the new, angular body for that year – the brushed aluminium is still there, in a panel along the upper body sides. The greenery behind is the open space at the centre of Grosvenor Square.

Plate 206   1963 Oldsmobile Starfire. Convertible version of the Starfire for '63, this smart gold soft-top was captured in Hertford Street, close to the London Hilton Hotel. The old 394 engine would survive another year, to be replaced in 1965.

Plate 207   **1963 Oldsmobile F-85 DeLuxe.** For '63, F-85 took on a new, more angular look to stay in theme with the full-size cars, looking much bigger than the previous models although wheelbases remained at 112 inches. This very smart '63 wagon, with its tow-bar and knobbly rear tires, was spotted in a back street somewhere down Hammersmith way.

Plate 208   **1963 Oldsmobile F-85 DeLuxe.** I spotted this sedan almost as I stepped out of Liverpool Street Station one day – it is taking off from the traffic lights in Bishopsgate, in the City. I've no idea where those number plates hale from!

Plate 209   **1964 Oldsmobile Super 88.** This '64 Holiday Sedan, spotted parked in Stratton Street, which is a side turning off of Piccadilly, shows the even more restrained restyle of the '63 bodyshell. Super 88 was now down to only four-door models, presaging its complete demise for '65.

Plate 210   **1964 Oldsmobile Dynamic 88.** The Dynamic 88 was now the backbone of Olds production; this is the long and angular station wagon version. I can't help but wonder if they had towed that trailer all the way from Nevada?

Plate 211   1964 Oldsmobile F-85 DeLuxe. Along with other GM compacts, the F-85 effectively moved up into the intermediate category for '64, using the new A-body shell shared with Special/Skylark, Chevelle and Tempest/LeMans. The 215 was dead, to be sold on to Rover a few years later – engines now were a Buick-built V-6 or the new 330-cid iron-block V-8.

Plate 212   1964 Oldsmobile Starfire. Starfire was still there as the performance full-size entry, although a new Jetstar I hardtop offered a similar package at a lower price. The aluminium side panels were gone now, to be replaced by a cleaner appearance with uncluttered body sides.

Plate 213   1965 Oldsmobile Delta 88. Delta 88 effectively replaced the old Super 88 for '65 – new bodies showed a dramatically sleek turn on the 'big-hips' look which was becoming fashionable. The new engine for full-size Olds' was the 425 cubic inch V-8, standard in all models except for the Jetstar 88, which, as low-price car, fitted the F-85's 330-cid unit. This is clearly another embassy car – Burma, this time!

Plate 214   1965 Oldsmobile F-85 Cutlass. Carrying over the '64 A-body with this neat restyle, the '65 Cutlass remained the sporty, top-price version of Oldsmobile's intermediate – this one is parked on familiar territory, outside the US embassy.

Plate 215   1965 Oldsmobile VistaCruiser. In mid-64, Buick and Olds introduced a special wagon version of the A-body cars; Buick's Sportwagon and the Olds VistaCruiser sat on a longer, 120-inch wheelbase and shared the raised rear roof section, with its peripheral 'skylight' glazing. Both proved to be popular, remaining in the line-up for many years, although neither were ever common, in my experience, in the UK.

Plate 216   1966 Oldsmobile Jetstar 88. As mentioned above, Jetstar 88 had become the low-price full-size Olds in '64. This '66 model sedan, on the Park Lane giratory loop, demonstrates the last of the line – the Delmont 88 took over the mantle in '67.

123

Plate 217   1966 Oldsmobile Delta 88. Mid-price backbone model of the Olds line-up was still the Delta 88 in '66, and would remain so for some years to come. Were the Swiss owners of this four-door on holiday, with that well-loaded roof rack?

Plate 218   1967 Oldsmobile Toronado. Toronado, using the Buick Riviera's bodyshell, first appeared for 1966; but the Toronado had the Olds 425 engine coupled to a front-drive arrangement where the transmission lay alongside the engine-block. In 1969, Alec Issigonis, designer of the BMC Mini, was quoted as saying that front wheel drive would never be practicable with bigger than two-litre engines…!

Plate 219   1954 Packard 400. Despite their one-time popularity with British buyers, Packards were a rarity by the time I was taking pictures in the sixties. I found this very sad looking '54 convertible in the car park at Earls Court, I think at the 1967 Motor Show. This was the last year of the big 359 cubic inch straight eight – solid, robust, but by then very unfashionable!

Plate 220   1953 Packard Clipper DeLuxe. Clipper was Packard's lower-price car, on the shorter 122-inch chassis, and using a smaller 327-cid eight-cylinder engine. There were a few Clippers around London even then – I do have other pictures, which will appear in later volumes – when I shot this sedan on Park Lane about 1965.

125

Plate 221   1955 Plymouth Belvedere. Belvedere was in its second year as Plymouth's top model in '55, when it was graced with the clean, advanced styling of its new Exner body, and the option of the first V-8s, either 241 or 260 cubic inches. This was also the year of the push-button gearshift for the Powerflite Automatic transmission.

Plate 222   1958 Plymouth Belvedere. By '58, the Fury had appeared, but so far as the two-door hardtop only sports entry, available *only* in Ivory (Stephen King please note!). Belvedere remained the top-priced regular line, with its new quad-headlight front end treatment – Chrysler did sell its 'normal' cars for export as well as the oddball De Soto Diplomat, as this RHD car demonstrates.

Plate 223   1960 Plymouth Suburban DeLuxe. Plymouth, like a number of other manufacturers, sold its Station Wagons under different nameplates to the other passenger cars – the Suburban came in three price levels, of which the DeLuxe was the cheapest, utilising what would be Savoy trim in a sedan. The Custom was trimmed like a Belvedere, now the mid-price car, and the Sport Suburban echoed the Fury, now itself a full line of body types.

Plate 224   1962 Valiant V200. Plymouth, like its low-price rivals, had entered the compact car debate in 1960, with its conventionally-engineered but wildly styled Valiant. By '62, styling had been toned down a bit, as this quite neat two-door sedan shows – front ends picked up the trapezoid grille of the contemporary Chrysler, but with horizontally-mounted headlights.

Plate 225   1962 Plymouth Coronado. Many of Chrysler's export cars for Europe were assembled in Belgium from American-supplied components, and this allowed for the occasional odd variation. The Coronado was a stretched Plymouth, offered only in Europe – rather like the longer-wheelbase Mercedes' which became popular a good few years later.

Plate 226   1963 Plymouth Belvedere. Styling had become almost bizarre under Virgil Exner, but was becoming more conventional by '63, with Elwood Engle in charge. The short 116-inch wheelbase platform was shared with the regular Dodges, but there was no equivalent to the Custom 880 in Plymouth's line-up, and wouldn't be until '65.

Plate 227 **1964 Plymouth Fury.** Fury, as mentioned before, had become a full line in '59, with its sporty aspirations taken over by the Sport Fury, a situation which continued through 1964. Chrysler seemed to enjoy a bit of an export boom that year – I can remember quite a number of these right-hooker Furys around, and there was certainly an energetic sales campaign going on for the next few years.

Plate 228 **1964 Plymouth Sport Fury.** And, just to prove the point, here is the '64 Sport Fury! By now, only trim details, bucket seats and the spinner hubcaps distinguished the sporty variant – the mighty 426 hemi was an option that year, but, contrarily, most went into stripped-out Savoy sedans, to be used on the drag-strip!

Plate 229   1964 Plymouth Belvedere. Still at half-mast in the Plymouth line-up, this is the '64 Belvedere – these cheaper models were quite rare in England, because the importers always pushed the more pricey Fury. This one was parked in Goldhawk Road, in Shepherd's Bush, one day when I went to take a look at Cliff Davis Cars, whose premises are just out of shot in the background.

Plate 230   1965 Plymouth Sport Fury. Like Dodge, the Plymouth line-up underwent a drastic re-think for '65. The old, short-wheelbase car continued, carrying an expanded Belvedere line, as an intermediate, and this new, bigger Fury became the full-size Plym. Still top of the tree was the Sport Fury, seen here outside the US Embassy.

Plate 231   1965 Plymouth Fury II. Furys came as I, II or III, as well as Sport Fury, the different Roman Numerals delineating their status – and all wagons had carried the regular model names since 1962. The range of Fury engines was bewildering – standard in most was the 225-cid slant six, but top option was the RB-block 440, with a number of small-block and big-block choices in between.

Plate 232   1965 Plymouth Fury I. Cheapest of the Furys was a favourite with fleet operators at home, and even found some favour in a similar role here in the UK. This sedan was circulating in Grosvenor Square – we are looking Southwards, into North Audley Street, in the background.

Plate 233   1965 Plymouth Belvedere II. Like Fury, Belvedere now used Roman Numerals to define price level, but stopped at II – a sporty Satellite filled the top slot, in two-door styles only. This is the mid-price Belvedere II, cruising in the sunshine on Park Lane.

Plate 234   1966 Plymouth Fury III. This is the '66 version of the top-price Fury sedan, looking somehow rather up-market after its restyle, with the added fender skirts – the picture taken just yards from the last one, but under rather duller weather conditions!

Plate 235   1966 Plymouth Belvedere II. It was the intermediate's turn for an all-new body in '66 – Belvedere came out with these very straight lines, while Coronet, the Dodge version, had strongly-hipped lines (see plate 126). This car I remember as being in a rather dingy dark turquoise colour, while the old PA Cresta parked behind was in the lovely pink and grey finish that Vauxhall offered around 1959.

Plate 236   1966 Plymouth Valiant Signet. Valiant, too, had undergone a few changes over the years. The '66 continued a rather smart, squared-off body which had appeared first for '63 – Signet was the top-of-the-line, sporty variant, available only in two-door models. A fastback-roofed Valiant had been introduced to counter the Mustang in mid-64 with the name of Barracuda.

Plate 237   1967 Plymouth VIP. VIP had been added to the line-up for '66, as a kind of luxury equivalent to the Sport Fury. VIPs came in hardtop bodies only, either two- or four-door, and had more luxurious trim than any other Plym. This very smart '67 four-door is outside what was perhaps my favourite Hotel, the Grosvenor House.

Plate 238   1967 Plymouth Fury II. Mid-price Fury, these were again quite rare here – this one was, I think, awaiting delivery when I found it in an extensive holding yard in Earls Court one October. This was Motor Show time, 1967, and with it were a number of brand-new '68s, and a lot of the dubious Australian VE Valiant which Chrysler were attempting to sell here then.

Plate 239   1967 Plymouth Barracuda. For '67, Barracuda gained a hardtop and a convertible alongside the fastback – all carried completely restyled bodies on the new Valiant platform. This is the fastback version – engines ranged from the little slant six up to a high-output 383.

Plate 240   1968 Plymouth VIP. I mentioned just now the holding yard full of Plymouths which I found in October '67 – this, and the next two, are more shots I took that day. All the cars are obviously new imports, and most of them had yet to be stripped of the protective film over the paintwork – this is a four-door VIP…

Plate 241   1968 Plymouth Fury III. …and this is a Fury III wagon. The big Chrysler Station Wagons around that time had a truly massive appearance, partly the result of their styling, but also partly from the three-inch-longer wheelbase than the Fury sedan.

Plate 242   1968 Plymouth Sport Fury. Sport Fury was still there, although I suspect any real sporting pretensions had long been forgotten, the name now implying only a bucket-seat interior and a body clean of much of the bright trim found on regular Furys.

Plate 243   **1956 Pontiac Star Chief.** I remember taking this picture on one of my last trips into London, around 1969, which might explain the rather scruffy state of this originally-prestigious convertible. In '56, Pontiac was in the second year of their V-8 production; Star Chief was the top-price model, with the 227HP version of the 316-cid unit.

Plate 244   **1957 Pontiac Chieftain.** By contrast, this '57 is in much better condition, and taken under much nicer weather conditions, too! Chieftain was the cheaper line – for '57, a new mid-price car called Super Chief had also appeared, as had the first Bonneville, a convertible-only line with a fuel-injected version of the 347-cid V-8 which powered all Pontiacs.

Plate 245   **1958 Pontiac Laurentian.** From its exterior trim, you might suppose this to be a Star Chief – but the RHD configuration says that it has to be Canadian-built. Canadian Pontiacs were a bit like De Soto's Diplomat – actually Chevrolet chassis and bodyshell, with Pontiac exterior panels and trim, and sold in the UK as a result of the preferential duty on Commonwealth products.

Plate 246   **1960 Pontiac Bonneville.** Genuine US-built Pontiacs had a longer wheelbase for Star Chief and Bonneville – by '60, Bonneville was a full car line, including even a station wagon. This four-door Vista hardtop sedan manages to look huge, with its long, flat lines emphasised by the ubiquitous GM flat-top roof; engines were up to 389 cubic inches.

Plate 247   1962 Pontiac Bonneville. I always had a real soft spot for the '62 Pontiac – I can't say why, the styling just appealed to me, somehow. This superb convertible was parked on Park Lane, not far from the Dorchester – you just try leaving a car there, nowadays!

Plate 248   1962 Pontiac Tempest LeMans. Pontiac had acquired their own compact in '61, using the common GM A-body platform – the Tempest was unique, however, in mounting the transmission, manual or automatic, on the rear axle, and using a curved propeller shaft to lower the floor line. This is the '62 restyle, in soft-top form.

Plate 249   1963 Pontiac Bonneville. The new Pontiac for '63 looked pretty revolutionary when it was revealed – the dramatic stacked headlights were in distinct contrast to everyone else's style, and the clean lines and emphatic hip-line stood out from the crowd. This two-door hardtop was spotted in an underground car-park, in Grosvenor Square.

Plate 250   1964 Pontiac Grand Prix. The first Grand Prix had been introduced as a mid-62 model, with a distinctive grille and other styling accents, as a sporting variant based on the shorter Catalina platform. This '64 still shows the simple grille, with factory-added foglights, and clean trim-free lines which marked the GP; a bigger, 421-cid engine was now optional in full-size cars.

Plate 251   **1964 Pontiac Bonneville.** Top-price Pontiac wagon was still this Bonneville – this one appears to have suffered a slight ding in the rear fender! Regular Pontiacs for '64 had this rather fussy front end styling, lacking the sharp edges of the '63.

Plate 252   **1964 Pontiac Parisienne.** Still the common UK import was the Canadian-built Pontiac; North-of-the-border equivalent of the Bonneville was the Parisienne, although these were still based on Chevrolet running gear. This must have made life easier for the importers, with a common engine and trans, etc., with the RHD Chevvies they were also selling.

Plate 253   1964 Pontiac Tempest GTO. The first of the famous GTOs! Introduced in mid-64, GTO started a new performance formula, with its intermediate bodyshell fitted with a big-block V-8, and up-rated suspension and brakes to cope with the added power. Road tests confirmed its awesome capabilities, with 0-60 times as low as, if not lower than, any European sports car of the time. Engine, at this stage, was a 389.

Plate 254   1965 Pontiac Grand Prix. The new GM B-body for '65 looked very good on Pontiac, picking up the big-hipped lines of the previous models, and returning to the sharp stacked-lights front end of '63; the bull-nose dividing the grille also became even more emphatic. Grand Prix especially had real style, with its clean lines and unique concave-windowed roofline.

Plate 255   1965 Pontiac Bonneville. Bonneville, too, looked very sharp for the new year, although the damage to this convertible's rear fender suggests there might have been a drawback to the big-hips look! The greenery of Grosvenor Square makes up, again, the background to this picture.

Plate 256   1965 Pontiac Parisienne. More often seen in the UK, as always, was the Canadian product, this Parisienne four-door perhaps the most common of all. Imports usually had the Chevrolet 327 and Turbo Hydramatic 350 combination – the shop front behind leaves no doubts about where this was taken!

Plate 257   **1965 Pontiac Tempest GTO.**   Tempest had acquired stacked lights, grafted into the existing bodyshell, for '65, and GTO was no exception. The formula remained as before, with the big V-8 in a small, light car, and performance was as startling as ever – other manufacturers were on the bandwagon by now, but none ever achieved the notoriety of the GTO.

Plate 258   **1966 Pontiac Bonneville.**   The '66 restyle of the '65 body added shark-like curves to the grille area, making the new Pontiac a real stand-out in any crowd. This beautiful convertible in the familiar surroundings of Park Lane.

Plate 259   **1966 Pontiac Tempest GTO.** GTO remained officially part of the Tempest line until 1970 – '66 saw a new bodyshell, shared with the other GM intermediates, seen here in convertible form. Performance was as neck-snapping as ever, with the 360HP 389 engine.

Plate 260   **1966 Pontiac Tempest LeMans.** In the public perception, GTO seems to have overshadowed the regular Tempests, which were themselves exceptional and stylish cars, as evidence this smart LeMans four-door. And who remembers the overhead cam sixes? Introduced for '66, they used a special cylinder head mounted on a version of the Chevrolet straight six, with a belt-driven camshaft – performance was good, but a tendency to run cam bearings led to their demise after a few years.

Plate 261   1958 Rambler Ambassador. American Motors Corporation were also deeply into name games during the period we're dealing with – the old Nash and Hudson companies had merged in 1954, and those nameplates had vanished for '58. All cars were Ramblers, and top priced line was the Ambassador, here in Cross-Country station wagon form. During the sixties, sometimes car were sold as AMC, or under the separate model designations – I've listed them all under R for simplicity's sake!

Plate 262   1961 Rambler Classic DeLuxe. Classic was the regular full-size Rambler, even if it was really more intermediate in size – DeLuxe was the cheapest trim variant. A straight six was standard equipment, with two small V-8s optional – Rambler always enjoyed a degree of popularity in England, being seen as a car of trans-Atlantic style in a more European-sized package.

Plate 263   1964 Rambler Ambassador 990H. Ramblers were so common in the UK then, that I tended only to photograph the more unusual ones, or the new models as they appeared. This 990H hardtop was Rambler's mid-64 entry into the growing sporty hardtop field, with its blacked-out side trim and yellow-and-black paint scheme.

Plate 264   1965 Rambler Marlin. The Marlin took everyone by surprise – AMC jumping into the sporty-intermediate market was one thing, but to do it with such a superbly stylish package was not expected. Perhaps the prettiest of all the mid-size fastbacks, it was only let down by the use of standard Classic front-end sheet metal and grille styling.

Plate 265   1965 Rambler Classic 770. From '63, number designations had replaced the old DeLuxe-Super-Custom names in both Classic and Ambassador lines. 770 was top-price Classic – this two-door must have been registered early in the model year, to be wearing a late-1964 'B' plate.

Plate 266   1965 Rambler American 440. Rambler's compact, first in the field dating from 1958, was the American – by '65 it had evolved into quite a stylish little car, with the new straight six engines in 199 or 232 cubic inch sizes; this soft-top is a particularly pretty little motor.

Plate 267   1966 Rambler Classic 770. '66 saw only a minor restyle of the '65 cars. This is today's puzzle picture – the car is undeniably a '66 model, so why is it wearing a 'B' numberplate, which has to have been issued in 1964? And, I wonder, what ever happened to the District Bank Ltd?

Plate 268   1966 Rambler Classic 770. This two-door hardtop shows the same trim details as the station wagon above, along with the newly-restyled angular roofline of the two-door body, as compared with Plate 265.

Plate 269   1966 Rambler American Rogue. Rogue was the new top-price, sporty hardtop version of the little American, introduced for '66. Even then, no V-8 was available; top option was the 232 straight six.

Plate 270   1967 Ambassador 990. No longer carrying the Rambler name, Ambassador was sold at home as its own marque for '67, even though they came under the same banner here in the UK. Quite a number made their way to England, among them this four-door sedan, captured in my happy hunting ground of Park Lane.

Plate 271   1967 Rambler Rebel SST. New top-of-the-line models appeared for '67 – Ambassador had the DPL, and Rebel this sports-oriented SST, available as hardtop or convertible only. Although registered here in its year of manufacture, this soft-top is a US-built left hooker.

Plate 272   1967 Rambler American Rogue. The American kept its Rogue as top cat for '67, but now there was a convertible as well as the two-door hardtop – and at last there was a V-8 option, in the form of the all-new 290 cubic inch unit. Rebel and Ambassador had new engines too – the 290 or its bigger brother, the 343.

Plate 273   1954 Studebaker Commander. Studebaker's all-new styling took the automotive world by storm in 1953, with this sleek, low-slung body for all their two-door coupe or hardtop models. Credited rightly to Raymond Loewy, it is interesting to note that Virgil Exner worked on these cars too before joining Chrysler. Sedan models used a more upright version of the same style, giving better headroom – this is a V-8 Commander coupe, albeit with one headlight bezel missing!

Plate 274   1956 Studebaker Sky Hawk. For '56, regular Studebaker models had a new, more conventional body, but the old Loewy coupe continued in the form of the sports-slanted Hawks. All had this new, vertical grille arrangement, and more ornate body trim than before – this is the 289-cid V-8 powered model, regarded as part of the President range; Top cat was the Golden Hawk, with the big Packard 352 V-8.

Plate 275   1957 Studebaker Silver Hawk. The old Loewy body still went on for '57, and indeed for many years to come! The line was a bit simpler now – Silver Hawks had a choice of straight six or V-8 power, and the Golden Hawk a supercharged 289-cid unit in place of the heavy Packard unit; fibreglass fins changed the silhouette of the rear fenders for '57. Added, unoriginal lower-body trim doesn't help the appearance of this car.

Plate 276   1957 Studebaker Champion. The new sedan body underwent minor restyling for '57 – Champion was lowest-but-one in the line-up, with the Scotsman below it and the Commander and President above, and came with the old side-valve straight six engine. By a strange coincidence, both this car and the '58 in the next shot had badly damaged front ends, hence the rear-view pictures!

Plate 277   **1958 Studebaker Champion.** You get the impression that even as early as the late fifties, Studebaker were struggling for development funds – the restyle for '58 especially seemed to rely bits of metal or fibreglass stuck onto the existing body, like the fibreglass fins on the rear fenders, and the widened panels to accept quad headlights at the front, just visible in this rear shot.

Plate 278   **1960 Studebaker Lark VI Regal.** The car that almost saved Studebaker! They were quick to spot the possibilities of the compact car market, first exploited by Rambler, and came out with the Lark line in 1959. Based around the existing central box of the old Champion, with much abbreviated front and rear ends, the Lark was a solid, reliable, economical car which revived the company's fortunes for a number of years. Detail changes only separated this '60 Regal convertible from its '59 counterpart; wheel covers aren't original!

Plate 279   1960 Studebaker Lark VI Regal. The use of Roman Numerals designated the use of six-cylinder or V-8 power in the Lark – the only way I know to tell a '60 from a '59 is that the little oval Lark badge is in the bottom centre of the grille – '59s had it tucked into one corner.

Plate 280   1961 Studebaker Hawk. Yes, that old '53 body was still around! By '61, the Hawk was down to a one-car line, in the form of this still-stylish-looking coupe – engine choices were now two versions of the 289-cid V-8, and the fibreglass fins are still there.

Plate 281   1963 Studebaker Avanti. The real thing! No Chevrolet-powered, late-model look-alike, this is the genuine article, a '63 Avanti, in the gold livery which was used on all the press cars at its release in mid-62. For a company already struggling financially, the Avanti was a bold chance to take – a serious performance contender, with its radical styling and fibreglass body, it did more for Studebaker's prestige than it did for the balance sheet, unfortunately – less than five thousand were built in total.

Plate 282   1963 Studebaker Lark Cruiser. With their compact size, and reputation for solid reliability, Studebaker enjoyed relatively good sales in the UK at times, even as their share of the home market was dwindling. This is a RHD import version of '63's top-line sedan, the Lark Cruiser, which came as standard with the 289 V-8.

Plate 283   1963 Studebaker Lark Daytona. The attempt on the performance market showed through in some of the late model names – Daytona designated the sporty variant, in two-door hardtop or convertible form, although, perversely, it also offered a station wagon! Again, you will note that this car is right hand drive.

Plate 284   1964 Studebaker Avanti. It seems appropriate to finish this selection of my pictures with such a rarity – only 809 Avantis were built in '64, its last year of production. The square headlight mountings mark this as a '64, although this detail was in fact an option for that year rather than standard equipment. Engines ranged up to 304 cubic inches, and top option offered a whopping 335 BHP with the aid of a Paxton supercharger.

Conclusion

Well, there you have it – the first nearly-three-hundred pictures from my old collection; I hope you have enjoyed them! As I have said before, if this volume is well received, I will offer a further selection in the future – I'm not sure, at this time, if it would be best to continue with the London pictures, or, for the sake of variety, to pick a few hundred from the Oxford shots. You'll have to wait and see!

Acknowledgments

There are a number of people I should thank, not so much for help in preparing this volume, but for their sharing of my enthusiasms over the years – those who employed me in the American car trade: Chris Frost, of C.M.Frost Auto Parts, Dave Riswick, Melvyn 'Woody' Wooding and Ian Messenger, all of John Woolfe Racing in the 1970s. My work colleagues of that period, some of them still in the business today: Steve Trice, Pete Stafford, Stu Bradbury, Lynda Francis, and so many others… And friends gained along the way, customers and fellow-lovers of 'Yank-Tanks', too numerous to mention individually; except perhaps for Phil Wadsworth, a friend for thirty years now, who has done much to support and encourage me in a number of endeavours, including this latest! I have done most of the work on this book myself, but my thanks have to go, in that respect, to Roger Wickham of Amherst Publishing, who has not only enthusiastically supported the project but handled all the page-setting and production of this volume. And I have relied upon Richard M. Langworth's 'Encyclopedia of American Cars' to support my own knowledge of the subject at frequent intervals along the task of writing of the captions. My thanks to all of them – and to all of you enthusiasts, who keep the American car alive on the roads of Great Britain.

Steve Miles
September 2004

LIMITED EDITION PRINTS

Overall size:

16 x 12 inches

approx 40 x 30cm

£34.95 each incl.

FREE P & P

within the UK

Limited edition prints are available direct from the publisher.
All prints are individually numbered and signed, card-mounted, and framed.
A maximum of fifty copies of each picture will be produced for sale.

How to order:
Please send your choice of plate numbers, your name and address,
and a cheque or postal order in full payment (£34.95 each) to:
SGM Publishing, Cosgrove Wharf, Lock Lane, Cosgrove, Northants MK19 7JR

CALENDARS

The OVER HERE 2005 calendar contains thirteen superb
black and white photographs of American classic cars taken
from OVER HERE Volume 1. Available now from your usual
supplier, or direct from the publisher for only £9.95 each (UK).

The OVER HERE 2006 calendar will contain another thirteen
superb black and white photographs taken from OVER HERE
Volume 2. Available in October 2005 from your usual supplier,
or direct from the publisher for only £9.95 each (UK).

SGM Publishing, Cosgrove Wharf, Lock Lane, Cosgrove, Northants MK19 7JR

OVER HERE Volume 2

Another collection of rare historic photographs of American cars on the streets of England,
this time taken around the lovely city of Oxford. Volume 2 of Steve Miles' photographic
collection is expected to be ready in the spring of 2005 - for the latest information, contact
the publisher, as above, or check our website at www.sgmpublishing.co.uk.